Enoch Calendar 5947 A.M. 2022/2023 A.D.

Kenneth B. Jenkerson

Enoch was given these Instructions by YAH! To Have a Solar Calendar Year consisting of 364 days. 12 months of 30 days each with 4 Intercalary Days known as the 2 solstices and the 2 equinoxes we have annually. YAH has His own Holidays carved into this calendar- which I think both of which will be kept throughout eternity.

Jeremiah 6:16 "Thus says Yah, Stand by the ways and see and ask for the ancient paths, Where the good way is, and walk in it, and you shall find rest for your souls! But they said, "We will not walk in it!!!"

Preface

These Appointed Times of YAH are part of His instructions to us on how to please Him and how to walk in His ancient paths. He tells us not to learn the way of the gentiles. The majority of the holidays on our gentile calendar known as the Gregorian calendar have pagan origins into gentile practices that we as Believers in YAH and His only begotten Son. Valentines Day, Easter, Halloween, Thanksgiving, Christmas all gentile practices with pagan origins. Not only are we commanded to stop celebrating these days, but we are also commanded to keep YAHs Holidays (Holy Days) or Appointed Times. Most of us don't even know about them, but most of them are listed in Leviticus 23 and Numbers 28 and 29. However, there are a few hidden ones that you have to dig for or have revealed to you, but I assure you they are there! This Calendar is based of the Calendar found in the Qumran Caves in the Essenes Community.

May we all learn to study to show ourselves approved unto YAH. May we all learn how to prove that which is pleasing to YAH and may we learn to love YAH with all that is in us and may we learn to love each other at the level we are at. May we learn how to produce good fruit that will remain which I think is done through the process of making disciples who are able to reproduce in others what YAH has produced in them. I have many teachings available on my website at http://disciplemakingpastor.org I also have a You Tube channel called Ken Jenkerson currently with 69 videos of teachings. My email is kenjenkerson@Yahoo.com if you wish to contact me. May YAH bless you and keep you; May YAH make His face shine on you and be gracious to you; May YAH lift up His countenance on you and give you peace. Shalom- Ken Jenkerson

MatithYahu 3:3
"The voice of one crying in the wilderness, Make ready the way of YAH, Make His Paths Straight!"

Come out of Babylon My People!

Table of Contents

Preface………………………………………….……

Table of contents………………………….…..……..

Urgent Situation Update for 2022 A.D…..I-XXVII

Understanding the Calendar……………..…1

A list of the Creators Holidays…………....11

Names of Months found in Scripture……..15

Twelve Month Calendar begins:

First Month……………………………….16

Second Month……………………………17

Third Month………………………….....18

Fourth Month…..19

Fifth Moth……………………………...…20

Sixth Month……………………..….........21

Seventh Month..……………….…….…..22

Eight Month……………………………...23

Ninth Month …………………………...24

Tenth Month…………………….....…..25

Eleventh Month………………………...26

Twelfth Month…………………………....27

URGENT!!!
Current Events Update: 2022 A.D. / 5946A.M.

Buckle Up! The Tribulation is Here! The Great Tribulation Awaits! The Powers of the Universe are on Display, For all who have eyes to see and ears to hear! The Spirit and the bride say come! Behold He cometh quickly! Prepare Ye The Way! The voice of one crying in the wilderness, Make ready the way of Yah, make His paths straight! Come out of Babylon My people!!! Blow the Shofar, Sound the Alarm!!!

So just how quickly can we expect the Messiah to return? I dare say sooner than I ever imagined! I never imagined that I would live through the tribulation, but it's here already and moving with great speed unlike anything we could imagine. The forced vaccination, which isn't really a vaccination. Yes they (FDA) changed the definition of vaccination from Immunity to

Protection, because these vaccines don't provide immunity, they are not really vaccines, just this year 2021 they did this! This is obviously a pre-cursor to the Mark of The Beast- it's already that way for some in other parts of the world. Please Don't take the Death Jab. These Shots are not for the benefit of anyone's health. Rather they are the tools of Biological warfare! Yes, good people of the World- We are at WAR!!! The War on Humanity is here! The Devil wants to Kill, Steal, and Destroy!!! I am all for Science and proven vaccines! I am for life, pro-life, pro-human. I love America, the land that I love, the only land I have known; but our Demise is certainly here. Even if there were a civil war or an uprising of overthrowing our evil government officials; I don't think all of them are individually evil but as a whole it's Evil, if there were a civil war before the winter of 2022 A.D. I don't think it will work as far as altering the fulfilling of prophecy laid out in Revelation and Daniel and Matthew and Zechariah and Enoch. I think America is the second beast in Revelation 13:11, and Rome is the first beast in Romans 13:1. Maybe Rome is the iron in the 4th kingdom mentioned in Daniel and America is the clay. Maybe America will be able to have a refuge city or state for the unvaccinated, but I don't think so. This New World Order, One World Government is going to be the most tyrannical and destructive force of nature known to mankind's history. It's being ran thru the United Nations as the Head, but the money comes from various sources like the Pope, Jesuits, Vanguard, Blackrock, Bush, Queen of England the Royal Family, Prince

Charles, the Rothchilds, Rockafellers, Morgan, Kissinger, etc. who did I leave out? Vanguard and Blackrock own everything in America, and those families are the private shareholders of Blackrock and Vanguard. These people make up what's called the Builder Berg Commission and the Foreign Relations Committee. Klause Schwab is the president of the BBC and he is a main speaker for the NWO. A bunch of rich people who get together every couple of years to determine how they will rule the world!

At War with New Word Order and American Government

Separation of Church and State/Sunday Law Coming!

Make no mistake about it friends, America is at WAR!!! We are at war with our own government. Watch out, once they remove "Separation of Church and State" which they are trying to do now! They will make us like Rome in doing so! They will then enforce a "Sunday only" Worship Law and when we Sabbath Keepers don't go along they will kill us. When the worldly, unreligious people don't go along they will die. They are bringing in Digital Drivers licenses with our Vaccination Records and Social Credit Score on them. There will be no way to buy sell or trade with out bowing down and taking the Vaccination. Which is nothing more than MRNA- DNA gene altering gene therapy, Nano bite technology meant to remove the Name of YAHU written in your DNA and alter you. They are

Spike Proteins! They cause many health problems, blood clotting and heart attacks amongst the blatant common ones! They put baby stem cells from aborted babies in these shots! They can put luciferase in them which causes the skin to glow, They want to use 5g to connect to us through Wi-Fi. 5G penetrates the skin it's bad for us and will cause cancers. 5G will put us in a microwave and cook us. We won't even need the smart phone to have internet connections! They actually want us all hooked up to their Artificial Intelligence Brain (main CPU) within 9 years! The way I spell Anthony Fauci M.D. in Hebrew equals 666! He definitely is an evil man. If I had to guess who is the actual Man of Sin to be revealed as the Anti-Messiah standing in the Sanctuary declaring himself the be the Creator, the Abomination of Desolation. I would not be surprised if Obama resurfaces as the Head of the U.N. or the Head of the New World Order at least in our part in America. Using an English gematria Obama's name equal 666 and has many relationships to evil. The latest news is about terraforming. Our government is building machines to suck the CO2 right out of the air and store it underground. Bill Gates also is funding putting some type of particles into the atmosphere to block out the sun. They want to destroy Crops and Photosynthesis. They have engineered global starvation by cutting off supply lines, shutting down truckers, shutting down oil lines, shutting down coal, and shutting down society in general with covid lockdowns. Australia is in dire straights cause the have no guns to defend themselves. Canada is making laws so you can't speak out against vaccines, or you go to prison. China is threatening to take Taiwan. The world is in a mess with astronomical consequences coming. So, we are at War with our government. Every nation is at war with their own governments. Our governments are trying to implement the New World Government. We are at war with our own government, and we are at war with the New World Government!

War With China

We are at war with China. The Chinese government has a 40 year plan to destroy America. The next step on their plan which coincides with the NWO plan, is Crisis. So the Crisis that has been engineered is food shortage and it is coming. When they stopped making coal this year they impacted the Fertilizer which is tied into the Coal. No Fertilizer for farmers next year, along with the Supply line shortage created by our government- Scientists are saying our Food Supply might not recover until 2024 and that's not going to be true if they commence with terraforming. I honestly think we are being controlled by China already. It feels like communist China to me anyway. There is no free Speech in this country, if you can shut down President Trump when he is president, then there is no more free speech. Big Tech manipulates their social media platforms, and they are backing the NWO plans. You can't speak out against Vaccines, Transgenderism, Homosexuality, Lies. You can only spread misinformation and lies nowadays. The Media in America is just like in China! Yes our Media is owned by these rich pricks. Fox sometimes has some descent news with Tucker, but **you have to go to Independent News Reporters to get the truth** nowadays! A lot of media disinformation and information wars going on! Mike Adams is the founder of brighteon.com a YouTube replacement platform. On brighteon.com you can browse channels go to Info Wars with Alex Jones, or HRR (Health Ranger Report) with Mike Adams. There are others out there, but you can't trust CNN, MSNBC, NBC, CBS etc. the mainstream media is all owned by BlackRock and Vanguard! China is threatening to take Taiwan if they do World War 3 will break out Cause We need Taiwan so does Japan and many other countries. China may even invade America with troops. After we kill each other off this winter because of starvation and freezing. They could bomb us or emp knock out our power grid. If they do invade us, I think they will wait until we are in a much worse position than we are at the moment in November of 2021. But China has troops in Mexico and in Canada which to me says they will invade. Maybe they will help the U.N. Military that I'm sure will be here at some point. What is with all the FEMA camps in America with millions of stackable coffins in place and guillotines. Yes they plan on rounding us up and putting us in **FEMA camps, just like Auschwitz only a larger scale.** The One World Government will be responsible for the death of billions. Thanks to Bill Gates and Fauci these death shots will kill many. The ones who refuse will at some point be taken to FEMA and murdered for not being in compliance to an evil tyrannical reign of the Devil on Earth!

Spiritual War

We are in a Spiritual War. Yes we are! Lets see if we can determine where in Revelations we might be! Lets start with the Enochian Calendar. First of all if you have limited yourself to only reading the bible, as I did for many years, then you need to recognize that there are books that were left out of the bible because of hidden agendas! If the book of Enoch, Jubilees, or the Testament of the Patriarchs were in our bibles, then we would know that the Lunar Calendar is a sinful fallacy. We would know that the calendar the Jews use today is in FACT wrong! There is more Christian doctrine in Enoch than all the New Testament put together, there is more Christian doctrine in the Testament of the Patriarchs then in the NT. People READ the Dead Sea Scrolls at least!!! The Sons of Darkness (lunar calendar) lose to the Sons of Light (Solar Calendar) in the end times battle- just read the War Scrolls! I imagine Eternity will be a lifetime of learning! Why not start learning His Ways Now! The Ways of Christianity are not His!!! Christianity has one thing right that I see- they have the heart issue right! It's a heart issue- The Father is searching our hearts not our minds. Most of us probably are wrong in our ways because His ways are not our ways. I've been trying to learn His ways for a lifetime and I probably still don't have much of anything right from a knowledge standpoint. It's about a relationship with the Father and this Christianity has right and it might be the main issue anyway! His people perish for a lack of knowledge of Torah! If you can't prove it in the Scriptures, then you have no proof! Where did Yah change the Sabbath from the 7th to the 1st day? I can show you who and where it was changed! It was the Catholic Church my friends around 300 A.D.- we have inherited lies from our Fathers! In the last days 10 men will grab the garment of a Jew and say let us go with you for we have heard that Yah is with you. The real war is spiritual. It's a war for your soul. No soul who takes the Mark of the Beast will spend eternity with Yah! The enemy is looking to devour us but the battle belongs to Yahuah! It's not by might nor by power but by the Spirit of Yah! We just worship Yah and obey singing glory and honor power and strength to Yahuah. Let the Salvation of Yah be revealed! Don't let the devil creep into your heart!

Enoch Calendar and the Messiah return in the year 6000

The Enoch Calendar is in the year 5946 exactly 164 years ahead of the current year on the mainstream Jewish calendar. These 164 years. The standard dating of the destruction was 586 BCE. However according to classical Jewish chronology, the date of the destruction of the First Temple was 422 BCE. There is a period here of 164 years! Get the Picture? Currently Jews are lying, or they are deceived themselves, about the date of the calendar by 164 years, the exact difference between the accurate Enoch Calendar (Dead Sea Scroll Calendar) used by the Essenes of who John the Baptist was the leader; and the present lunar calendar used by mainstream Judaism. It was common practice for the Head of the Essenses to have 12 disciples and for the leader to have 30 disciples. Exactly the number Yahusha and John had. I think John was actually in the true bloodline to be the next High Priest- I recall his dad Zechariah was the High Priest when he was told John would be born to prepare the way for the Messiah! The Enoch Calendar is in the Year 5946 A.M. and the theology that comes from the dead sea scrolls from the Melchezidek document and the School of Aliyahu (Elijah), and the Essenes. The year of the world is 5946 and the theology says in the year 6000 the Messiah will return. 54 years away from the return of the Messiah! When I first came across this material around 2018, I had never before that thought that I would be around for the end of days. And then the corona virus hit and now the real disease is here the mark of the beast in the form of a vaccine! If this Enoch Calendar and theology is correct then we have about 54 years of this persecution to endure. After the events of late with the Corona Virus and the emergence of the Mark of the Beast and the New World Order looking to take over; I can now imagine that 54 years seems a long ways away and maybe the year 2032 is a more ideal timeline. In 54 years it will be 2075 A.D. or 2000 years ago the second temple was destroyed in Jerusalem by Rome. So, what if the theology is off and it's not based on the destruction of the temple but the death of Messiah in 2032. Maybe their Dead Sea Scroll Enochian Calendar is off a little. I don't think so! I think their calendar is right, I think their theology is right, I think the Messiah might return sooner than the 6000 Years to Save mankind from total annihilation. He says those days would be cut short if not, no life would have been saved! So where are we at in the book of Revelation and what happened to the rapture? I wonder what the Rapture Preachers are saying now- I hope by now they see the error of their doctrine and are beginning to teach truth rather than misleading the sheep with misinformation telling them peace when destruction is nigh! Buckle up friends the only ones getting taken away are the evil ones- I'm inheriting this planet!!! More than that my inheritance is the writings of the Patriarchs from Enoch to Jacobs sons this is my inheritance! Torah, the Messiah is my inheritance. I am His and He is mine! The Rapture gives a false pretense that we will be caught up into the heavens without dying and without going through the tribulation. But the New Testament says it is appointed unto every man to die once and then the judgment. Sorry guys no free passes, we all must face death; hopefully on the other side we will be able to say where is your sting O Death! The Rapture theology can leave one unprepared to go through the tribulation and bitter for having been lied too.

The Rapture?

Revelations 4:1 talks of John being called up to heaven, and I have heard many a preacher teach that this is the rapture and that the sequence in Revelations is in chronological order. Well guess what? Yep they were wrong, in my opinion! I think we are in Revelations 6 so what happened to the rapture in chapter 4? Besides the Bible says it is appointed unto all men to die once, and then the judgment! How can the rapture theory get around this verse? The rapture is the idea of not having to go through the tribulation, not having to die doesn't line up with scripture! Only two men have had this rapture experience and they will come back probably just as they went but they will come back to die in order to fulfill scripture.

1st Horse, White, The Conquerer

Revelations 6 - <u>The 4 horses!</u> I think the first horse already came. I think the second horse is currently here now and men will slay one another beginning this winter if not shortly thereafter. Just what I think, I have been wrong before! So I think <u>The first horse, the white horse, the conquering one</u> showed up on the scene and not everybody recognized him! I think it very well could have been Obama. Many Bible Scholars conclude that the Anti-Messiah is Muslim and will control the Muslim army in the end to come against Jerusalem in the final battle and while Jerusalem is being destroyed and all seems hopeless- the true Aleph Tav Messiah will appear and destroy the armies of evil and lock up the Devil for 1,000 years! I can see this being Obama. My wife's aunt dreamt that Obama was the Anti-Messiah back when he was first became President of the U.S.A. I've no reason to doubt her, she truly has a connection with the Father. So what if it isn't him, maybe it was the new world order making their move on us with the Covid Lock Down Restrictions that are still in effect in some places. I know I sure felt conquered. Curfews, couldn't travel except for Essential work; I'm surprised they let us go grocery shopping. How easy would it be for them to cut off the trucking industry that trucks food to everyone in the U.S.

2nd Horse, Red, War

I Think <u>the second horse, the red horse, the horse of war is here now</u> and could be identified as the vaccine. It's a death shot! They have declared war on us and our children. 28 million children are getting a shot that we are consenting too, this is outrageous! Hitler is going to look like a saint compared to the Eugenics, Sterilization, DNA altering nano tech they are distributing through these vaccinations of biological warfare. We have been set up to kill one another from starvation which our governments have engineered. <u>Revelation 6:4 "Men will slay one another" – that's the red horse of war!</u> World Starvation is on the way! Also don't forget bill gates is now going to be putting nano particles into our food and want to eliminate real meat at some point.

3rd Horse, Black, Famine

Oh wait that's the third horse, Famine! <u>The third horse, Famine, the black horse Revelation 6:6 "A quart of wheat for a days wage,</u> and three quarts of barley for a days wage, and do not harm the oil and the wine!" Famine is coming do what you can to prepare for the short and long run! Time to start planting trees, tilling the garden, building green houses, plant a perennial garden! Do what you can to be self sufficient in food. Learn how to can your food and preserve it.

4th Horse, Sickly Pale, Death

<u>The fourth horse is death, on an ashley sickly pale horse.</u> The ashen horse has a rider named Death and Hades was following with him and authority over ¼ of the earth is given to kill with sword, famine, pestilence, and wild beasts. These horses are referred to as seals, that was the first four seals. **<u>The fifth seal is Martyrs</u> which looks like will be the case for the unvaccinated!** The unvaxed will be forced out of society to survive and many will be martyrs. They will round us up and throw us in Fema Camps here in America just like they are doing in Australia and New Zealand right now. If we don't co-operate and be re-educated then off to the guillotines. Or maybe they will just lie to us and tell us there is food there and as desperate as we will be to eat we will go. Have the resolve of Daniels friends- Hananiah, Mishael, and Azariah "Even if Yah

does not deliver us, still we will not bow down to your false god". I think these will be the Elect and the Righteous. Unless these overall days of tribulation and great tribulation are cut short not even the Elect will survive! I interpret the Righteous and the Elect mentioned in Enoch and the New Testament as 2 groups. The elect are in relationship with the Creator but their ways are wrong, they don't have proper knowledge. The righteous are those who are in relationship with the Father and know His ways not only through Torah but through Oral Torah. Their ways are Yahs ways. I think there are 2 righteousness! One that comes from keeping the commandments of Torah- Luke 1:7. One that comes from grace freely given by the Messiah. **The sixth seal is that of terror! You will know you when we are here** because its astronomical! The Sun will become black and the moon like blood, stars will fall to the earth, every mountain and island will be moved out of their places!!! Men will hide themselves in the caves and rocks of the mountains and say to the rocks and mountains Fall on us and hide us from the presence of Him who sits on the throne, and from the wrath of the Lamb, for the great day of their wrath has come, and who is able to stand!!! I think it's interesting that Bill Gates has a terraforming project of shooting particles into the atmosphere to blacken out the sun! Gates also wants to set up machines in North America that will suck the CO_2 right out of the Air, which will cause life to die on the planet. Surely we will be able to recognize that sign and seal number 6! It starts off with a great earthquake which could be a reference to the

Chinese making an earthquake to cause a tsunami that can wipe out the East Coast of America, which some say they are currently trying to do.

144,000 Sealed/Multitude from the Tribulation

In Revelation 7 there is a remnant of Israel 144,000 sealed and a multitude from the tribulation- this chapter gives me great hope for the people! I think these are the righteous who know Yah and His True Ways and Keep them. I think they are the Kabbalist. There is a multitude which no one could count from every nation and all tribes and peoples and tongues standing before the throne and before the Lamb and they fall on their faces and worship!!! A great multitude of us we win this battle, of course in order to win you may have to lose your life!

Third of earth, trees, grass, sea, sea creatures, ships, stars, rivers, springs, sun, and the moon are destroyed 1/3

Revelation 8 is <u>the seventh seal which contains the seven trumpets. The first</u> is hail and fire mixed with blood, and a third of the earth is burn up, a third of the trees, and all the grass. <u>The second</u> trumpet is something like a great mountain burning with fire was thrown into the se and a third of the sea became blood and a third of the creatures died and a third of the ships destroyed. <u>The third</u> is a great star falls from heaven burning like a torch it falls on a third of the rivers and the springs of water, the star is called wormwood, and a third of the waters became like wormwood, and many men died from the bitter waters. The fourth trumpet is a third of the sun and the moon and the stars are smitten so that a third of them might be darkened and the day might not shine for a third of it and the night in the same way.

Locusts with faces of Men/ a third of mankind killed

Revelation 9 continues with the fifth trumpet. Locust come up out of the abys in the earth a bottomless pit and they have the power of scorpions, but they are told not to hurt the grass or any green thing nor any tree but only the men who do not have the seal of Yah on their foreheads. The locusts look like horses prepared for battle and on their heads crowns like gold and their faces were like the faces of men and they had hair like the hair of women and their teeth were like lions teeth with breastplate of iron and wings. I wonder if this has any relationship to CERN, and them attempting to make the god particle, using their star collider, slamming gasses and particles together trying to re-invent the big bang. I wouldn't be surprised if CERN which is in Houston Texas but is a European Organization for Nuclear Research, opens a door to a different dimension and demons come through it into our world. The sixth trumpet is the four angels bound at the Euphrates are released to kill a third of mankind and their army is 200 million horsemen and the horses have tails like serpents with heads to do harm. Fire, smoke and brimstone proceeds out of their mouths.

Two Witnesses

Revelation 10 and 11 <u>Here you get the two witnesses</u> who show up! It is appointed unto every man to die once and then the judgment. Only two men I know of who have not died are Enoch and Elijah! I suspect they are the two witnesses. They have the power to make fire proceed from their mouth. They have the power to shut up the sky so no rain will fall. They have power to turn water to blood and to smite the earth with every plague. The beast that comes out of the abyss will kill them and after 3.5 days they resurrect for men to see and then go up to heaven in the clouds in that hour a great earthquake happens and 7,000 people die. The seventh trumpet honestly I'm not sure but it looks like this is the coming of the Kingdom of Yah it's kind of vague to me anyway, along with Revelation 12. Revelation 12 part of it looks like what happened back in the beginning of time, when the devil fell from heaven. <u>Chapter 11:18 tells us He is coming back to destroy those who destroy the earth.</u> Well that's the entire agenda of the global warming agenda, ran by bill gates who wants to put particles in the air to block out the sun because the planet is to warm- which scientists say isn't true, we are not in need to blocking out the sun! But the Globalists, New World Order agenda is to depopulate the planet and destroy the planet. It's obviously demonic! Satan plans to kill us and the planet! Yah is coming back to save the planet and the entire solar system at that point, I would imagine!

The Mark of the beast

Rome the first beast

America the second beast

Revelation 13 this is the chapter where the mark of the beast is mentioned and the beast from the sea and the beast from the earth. The beast from the earth in verse 11 has tow hors like a lamb and speaks as a dragon. I think this is America. We say we are a Yah loving nation, but thy hypocrisy is overwhelming. We murder children with abortion day in and day out in this country, millions upon millions. We have a child and human trafficking government and Hollywood that abuses children, sacrifices them to the devil, and drinks their blood. Satanism is part of the new world order. There really is black magic being used today. There is also white magic if you will- power and miracles achieved by using Hebrew names of Yah. Black magic uses the same names only in the reverse for evil purposes- but there are spiritual powers at work that will be manifested in the near future. I won't be surprised if we see giants again. I'm sure you are all aware of the Afghanistan red headed giant of Kandahar that our military encountered and killed in 2002. The soldiers reported a grey cloud of smoke oozed out of the giant's mouth and formed into a sky demon. The demon warned the soldiers of an up-and-coming Jr. demon known as Barack Hussein Obama who would take power six years later in 2008 with a plan to destroy and bankrupt America. I don't know if it's true about the demon but I'm sure there are still giants dwelling in the Earth today. Well just recently they say our military encountered more giants in Afghanistan and that was part of the reason for the quick pull-out. I don't know for sure, but I think Biden pulled out to give it all the Al Qaeda and Chinese. Biden obviously is controlled by the NWO and by China. Biden is destroying America. Our borders have been flooded by terrorist lately so when they attack it shouldn't be too big of a surprise, right! The beast coming up out of the sea in verse one of Revelation 13, I think is Rome. Just imagine our pope and president working together to destroy probably in the name of saving the planet! So, if the mark of the beast isn't mentioned until Revelation 13 and we have not seen the before mentioned events leading up to this, so I conclude that the book of Revelation isn't in perfect Chronological order, at least not all of it, although parts of it may be. I think chapters 1-9 are in chronological order, but chapter 10-13 seem to fit in all over the place from the beginning of time to the end and then chapters 14-22 seem to fit the chronological order of things. So we may see some of the events of chapters 10-13 out of chronological order in my opinion. This is why we are seeing the mark of the beast in Revelation 13 being put into effect in Revelation 6 with the arrival of the 4 horses. I think Revelation 11:18 is appropriate in associating the New World Order agenda with scripture! It says He is coming to destroy those who destroy the earth! The globalists definitely have an agenda in place to destroy the earth! He will return to stop them!

Globalism uproots Socialism, Communism, and Capitalism

Daniel 7:8 speaks of a little horn that uproots 3 horns. The beast described is just like the beast in Revelation 13:1 the beast coming out of the sea. This little horn is the New World Government it is a Tyrannical Government. The 3 horns that it uproots are the 3 forms of government in each world government today. Socialism, Communism, and Capitalism. If you think Socialism, and Communism were bad wait until you get a personal experience with Globalism!!!

Tribulation/Great Tribulation

Math 24:6 "You will be hearing of wars and rumors of wars; see that you are not frightened". In verse 9 the Messiah says that "they will deliver you to tribulation and will kill you, and you will be hated by all nations on account of My name and at that time many will fall away and will deliver up one another and hate one another. Many will be led astray with Lawlessness and the love of many will grow cold. The one who endures to the end will be saved". But wait there's more this is just the tribulation! The Great Tribulation has yet to come! When you see the Abomination of Desolation standing in the Kadosh Place let those who are in Judea flea for the mountains. Pray that your flight may not be in the winter, or on a Sabbath (oh look what's still in place! Shabbat! It never changed it is the Seventh Day of the Week!) Remember they will make Sunday church a law it's gonna be legally required and your social credit score will be dunged if you don't go bow down to the Babylonian System! Ill not be surprised when the Sabbath, The Seventh Day Sabbath is outlawed. The Devil is ok with everything, except the right thing! Lawlessness will abound! Look at Verse 21 For then there will be a <u>great tribulation</u> such as has not occurred since the beginning of the world until now, nor shall ever be. And unless those days had been cut short, no life would have been saved; but for the sake of the elect those days shall be cut short. Then the Messiah shows up to save the day! When you see the leaves on the tree you know summer is nigh! Keep Oil in you lamps and extra oil for when you run out if He tarry!!! So we see there is tribulation which is where I think we are right now coming quickly upon us all around the world and very soon in full force in America- the land that I love. Once the New World Order is Established and the tyranny is in place with everyone being forced to take the mark; there will be another Temple built. Yes I think a third Temple will be built in Jerusalem and the Sacrifices restored or at least so the Lawless One can stand in the Kadosh place and take his seat in the temple of the Creator displaying and declaring himself as being the Creator. At this point the Great Tribulation will begin, Run for the Hills if you haven't already!!! So it gets so bad during the Great Tribulation that Those Days Are Cut Short! Maybe that's what's going on with the timeline on the Enoch Calendar; the calendar is accurate but if the Heavenly Father waits to send His son back to earth according to the 6000 years of mans rule, the man will perish! No one knows of that day and hour, not even the angels of heaven, nor the Son, but the Father alone! But I must declare that I see the leaves on the Fig Tree and Summer Draweth Nigh! Put Oil in your lamps and get plenty of extra Oil if He tarry, Yah be merciful to us in the end of days we beg of You!

Vaccines/ or Death Shots in the guise of Vaccines

I don't think the Vaccine is the actual mark but it's making a way for the mark which could actually be some chip, unless they have found a way around the chip which they may have with the vaccine, they can give you what's need to be hooked up to the internet without a physical device. I don't think they are putting that in the vaccines right now, I think they are only gene therapy, but that is the beginning of the process to get the mark without the chip. Who knows, I just heard today that they are going to be putting micro-chips into the vaccines. They are now going to be putting nano particles in our food and want to cut us off from meat eventually. We will have to grow our own food. If you have taken the vaccine and regret it, then I think there is still hope for you as far as it not being the mark of the beast yet and you can take some vitamins to try to combat what's going on in your immune system and pray and cry out to the Savior to

Save you and physically heal you. It's a Spiritual battle as much as a Physical one. Take these to help prevent getting Covid: Vitamin D3, K2, C, Zinc, Quercetin to help prevent getting Covid. Povidone Iodine nasal and throat spray is 99% effective in preventing sars 2 (covid). Also Quinine oral drops to help prevent Covid. So If you are sick with Covid you can take these: Prescription Ivermectin, and Hydroxychloroquine to help get over covid. Also MMS (Miracle Mineral Solution) otherwise known as Sodium Dioxide. To make Sodium Dioxide you need Sodium Chloride mixed with Citric Acid to make Sodium Dioxide to help prevent getting Covid and to get over it. You can order this Sodium Dioxide Kit on amazon. I have all of them except the Prescription ones Hydroxychloroquine and Ivermectin- good luck getting those! Although I have heard there is a list of doctors and pharmacist available online that you can get these products through and mailed to you- I don't have the list of available doctors or pharmacies sorry. If you have already taken the vaccines, you can take these to help combat it: Pomegranate, elderberry, chokeberry and green tea with egcg molecule to help combat vaccines taken. If there is a Small Pox Break out, as Gates has predicted, then there is a plant called Sarracenia Purpurea that will help get over it. I've gotten most this info from Doctors on Info Wars with Alex Jones and Health Ranger Report with Mike Adams on Brighteon. Dr. Zev Zelenko and Dr. Brian Ardis and Dr. Steve Kirsch and Dr. Sherri Tenpenny and Dr. Richard Fleming and Dr. Paul Cottrell and Dr. David Martin and Dr. Peter Breggin and Attorney

Thomas Renz and Dr. Judy Mikovits. We need to make sure we have oil in our lamps and learn from the parable of the fig tree. I would suggest doing what you can to secure food for the future, seeds, trees, perennial garden, garden. Non-Perishable food that will last for a long time. I would recommend having at least enough food stored up to get you through the winter and beyond if you can. Ultimately, we have to learn to put our Trust in Yahuah and let the chips fall where they may. But do what you can to prepare for the dark winter ahead and the emergence of the Mark of the Beast which means in order to be part of society you will have to take the mark. Develop communities now, off grid that can survive together without outside resources. They are going to come for the Doctors and Scientists first, then those who they have data on that shows they won't bow down to the system which is Babylon! They are keeping track of all of us already through social media platforms and everything you have ever done online, or on a smartphone offline as well. Don't trust the phones, the transmitter is activated when you turn the phone off. They hear everything and have algorithms set up to red flag certain things. If you speak out against them in any way they will come for you. It's a war against free speech and human rights but we must stand for what is right. May Yah give us the strength to endure to the end, and to endure well.

Economy:

The Economic state of our country is not good. Gas prices are soaring! $4.50 a gallon here right now! They are printing money like it's going out of style which is causing super-inflation. Their goal is to kill our Economy, not just ours either but on a global scale they are trying to destroy everyone's economy so they will have no choice but to get on board with a one world economy ran by the IMF which is ran by the UN, and the World bank which is ran by the Pope. They want a digital drivers license with a record of vaccinations and health and religion and a social credit score. They are going to carbon tax us and restrict our every movement just like they do in China. They shut down oil, coal, put heavy restrictions on trucking in California. They have no green mechanics in place to go green. Their whole green, save the planet agenda is actually, to destroy the planet and our economy and our constitution and our human rights and freedoms. They shut down our economy, sent everyone home, and cut off our supply lines. The economy is going to crash, our dollar will be no good soon enough. It will cost a days wage for a quart of wheat right here in America! Turn your dollars into actual product before this happens! I don't think the money in your account will be any good much longer! The market is going to crash in an instance overnight! Once Saudi Arabia decides to stop using the American dollar to trade the oil, it will be game over for the dollar! There is going to be some cyber attacks to kill small business and giver big business the monopoly. They are going to use cyber attacks to destroy bitcoin. Welcome to the Great Reset!

Borders:

They Biden regime have allowed lots of illegal immigrants across our borders recently, I want to say millions but I don't know the roundabout number. I don't know how many thousands of Afghanistan terrorists came over unvetted, but if they give each one who got separated from their kids under the Trump regime $450,000 then they will be funded as well! Mobs of immigrants flowing through American cities destroying them and raping our women! The southern border is infiltrated! And Biden wants more to come!

Schools/Education

Parents, it's time to remove your children from public schools and Christian Universities! They are brainwashing your children. The goal is to lead them astray from the truth! They are teaching perverted sexual material. From Fisting to f—king. sorry for the vulgarity but ya'll need to be woken up! That's Kindergarten and First grade material!!! The transgender, transhuman, homosexual predators are in charge of the doctrine that is being taught to our kids. If they are white they are being taught to hate themselves. If they are not white they are being taught to hate white people. They are calling trees racist. Critical race theory is garbage. Girls are being raped by men in their bathrooms now and it's ok legally. The days of Noah were probably not even this bad. You need to teach your kids, be very careful with social media platforms- this is another means through which kids are being attacked spiritually and mentally- they may seem innocent, but I guarantee you no man who has an ounce of integrity and worked on these platforms lets their kids on them because they know how evil it can be. There is an evil agenda for stealing our children, plus the schools are literally turning into vaccine clinics- just sending your kid to school is considered consent to the death jab!!! Bo Yahusha Bo!

The Disciple Making Pastor

Ken Jenkerson

11/13/21 A.D / 8/30/5946 A.M.

"Understanding the Calendar"

The Creators Calendar comes from the book of Enoch. The Heavenly Father instructs Enoch in many things. Enoch prophesied the end from the beginning and is credited with writing 366 books. 130 kings and princes of the world assembled to make Enoch their King. Enoch reigned 243 years and he taught them wisdom, knowledge, and the ways of Yah. In the 243rd year of Enochs reign, Adam died. Adam was buried by his two sons and Enoch and Methuselah. Enoch was teaching about 800,000 men at one time. All Christian doctrine that I am aware of comes from the writings of the Patriarchs who all seem to have been taught by Enoch and his son Methuselah before the flood, or by Noah and Shem who both learned from Enoch, after the flood. Abraham learned from both Noah and Shem. Abraham sent Isaac to the house of Shem and Eber to learn the ways of Yah and his instructions. Isaac sent Jacob, Esau refused to go, to learn from Shem and Eber. Jacob studied with Shem and Eber at the School of the prophets until the death of Shem in 2158 A.M. Eber continued the school, but copies of all of the records were given to Levi for safe keeping. This information can be found in the book of Jasher. I have read all 3 versions of Enoch and I only recommend the first Ethiopian version. Nothing contradicts scripture, it just complements it. In a book by Ken Johnson called the Ancient Order of Melchizedek the author points out that there are 10 Melchizedek priests with Messiah Yahusha being the 10th and final- I happen to agree with him. Melchizedek means king of righteousness, but it could also be translated as Melekzadok or king of the Zadok priests. The list of Melekzedek priests is Adam, Cainan, Enoch, Methuselah, Noah, Shem, Abraham, Isaac, Jacob, and then Yahusha. Jacob sent Levi to learn from Shem and the Levites were priests but not according to the order of Melchizedek. They were Levitical priests, Levi begat Kohath and Kohath begat Amram and Amram begat Moses and Aron. Amram would have had the writings of the Patriarchs and given them to Moses and Aron. So now we know where Moses got all his information for the Torah- the first 5 books of the bible. The solar calendar was kept from Adam to the time of the Maccabees when they agreed to change to a lunar calendar. The Zadokite priests during the time of Antiochus Epiphanes took the temple library to Qumran to protect the writings of the Patriarchs. The Zadokites will be the priest during the Millennial Reign of Messiah here on earth, at least that is the way I understand it to be- Ezekiel 48:11. If you take time to read Enoch or

Jubilees it exposes the deceit of the Levitical priesthood and what they have done with the Calendar of Yah. My opinion is that this is why they are not canonized. There are at least 141 references in the New Testament to the doctrine of Enoch and word for word quoted in Jude 14,15. These Zadokite priests split off from main steam Israel and went to the Qumran Caves taking the precious writings of the Patriarchs with them. The community called themselves Yahad or Yah is One or One Yah. They also called themselves New Damascus or Blood Heir. Psalms was the most popular scroll in the dead sea scrolls, but there were 15 copies of Jubilees and 10 copies of Enoch found amongst them so far. I recommend reading all the ancient dead sea scrolls you can get your hand on, but they all seem based off the ancient book of Enoch to me. So this is where the Enochian, Dead Sea Scroll, Essene, Zadokite, Torah, Solar, Creators Calendar comes from!

The Calendar is a solar 364 day calendar. It consists of 12 months of 30 days each. It contains 52 weeks.

It has 4 Intercalary days, Spring equinox, Summer solstice, Fall equinox, Winter solstice. In Hebrew there is one word for all four days- it's called a "Tekufa".

Every month has 30 days, with an "Intercalary Day" dividing each season = 364 days in one year.

The year always begins on the 4th day of the first month during the spring equinox, not after.

The Wednesday closest to the spring equinox is New Years Day or Aviv 1st or Beginning of the First Month!

The year always renews on the 4th day of the first month.

A.M. stands for Anno Mundi meaning the year of the world.

4 seasons of 91 days each. Every 3rd month has 31 days or the Intercalary day being the 31st day, change of the season. The Equinox or Solstice should occur on the Intercalary day. The day after (4th day of week) is the Head of Spring, Summer, Fall, and Winter. So you have 30,30,30,1; 30,30,30,1; 30,30,30,1; 30,30,30,1. It's important to note that when doing math you do not count the Intercalary day! So its 360 (days in a year). 360 x 3.5 years = 1,260 days.

It is interesting to note that the stars also confirm the calendar by giving us a different constellation each month for 12 months then starting over.

Quote from Ken Johnsons Book "Dead Sea Scroll Calendar" pages 5 & 6. "Most of us who study ancient history and church history in general, know about the modern Jewish Calendar. It is a lunar calendar consisting of 354-day year. Its months start on a new moon and every three to five years there is a leap month to keep it somewhat in sync with the four seasons. What we were never told is that there was another calendar; a solar one, used by the Essenes. This is their story. The Essenes taught that Yah gave us the perfect calendar. The base unit for the calendar was a twenty-four-hour day that was put in sets of seven, called weeks. Their calendar year was 364 days long, which evenly divided into 52 weeks. This made all holidays fall on the same day of the week every year! The Essenes said this calendar was observed unbroken from the time of Adam to Moses and down to the time of David. David wrote songs for each of the 52 Sabbaths of the year. We actually have some of those in the Dead Sea Scrolls! It remained the only calendar used by the Jews until the Greeks tried to force them to use the Seleucid Greek calendar. Unlike the 364-day solar calendar, this was a 354-day lunar calendar,. It changed New Years Day from the spring to the fall. It calculated the month, not by the solstices and equinoxes, but by the lunar new moon. The Maccabees rose up and drove out the Greeks. Antiochus Epiphanes died, and the new ruler was more interested in taxes than religion. Antiochus V Eupator made a deal with the Maccabees. <u>The Jews could keep their religion, but they had to pay tribute and to use the Seleucid Empire's calendar.</u> The Maccabees accepted the offer. If we believe the Dead Sea Scrolls, this is the true origin of the modern Jewish Calendar. The Zadok priest said that giving up the original solar calendar alone would be a grievous sin. Eventually the Zadok priests were driven out and settled in Qumran. They took with them copies of everything in the temple library."

I happen to think they started to convert the calendar to a lunar one during and after Babylonian captivity. After the Grecian Empire the Yah-given solar calendar with His Holidays seems to disappear completely from mainstream groups. With the exception of the Essenes and a group of Ethiopian Jews who have Enoch and Jubilees canonized in their bibles.

There is also evidence in the Dead Sea Scrolls that John the Baptist (YahuChannon the Immerser) was the leader of the School of prophets at the Qumran Caves in the Essene Community. There is a prophecy in their dead sea scrolls called community rule which declared one from their order would be the forerunner for the Messiah-Prepare Ye the Way of Yah, Make Straight His Paths. This was John the Baptist. John also had 30 disciples and the Messiah had 12 disciples. Correlating with 30 days in a month and 12 months in a year. This was an established Essene pattern of the Higher teacher having 12 and the lower teacher having 30 disciples.

According to the Talmud, Bavli Berachot 56-59, every twenty-eight years the sun returns to its original place when the world was created. This 28 year cycle is called the "Machzor Gadol" meaning "The Great Cycle".

The sun, moon, and stars were created on the 4th day of creation; therefore, the calendar starts on the 4th day of the week.

Revelation 11:3 & 12:6 both use 1,260 days which all theologians interpret as 3.5 years which all comes from the Enoch calendar and math. You cannot get 3.5 years matching 1,260 days exactly on anyone else calendar. 42 months times 360 days equals 1,260 days and 3.5 years on the Enoch Calendar.

Jubilees 2:9 "And Yah appointed the sun to be a great sign on the earth for days and for sabbaths and for months and for feasts and for years and for sabbaths of years and for jubilees and for all seasons of the years."

Jubilees 6:23-38 "And on the beginning of the first month, and on the beginning of the fourth month, and on the beginning of the seventh month, and on the beginning of the tenth month are the days of remembrance, and the days of the seasons in the four divisions of the year. These are written and ordained as a testimony forever. And Noah ordained them for himself as feasts for the generations forever, so that they have become thereby a memorial unto him. **And on the beginning of the first month he was bidden to make for himself an ark, and on that day the earth became dry and he opened the ark and saw the earth. And on the beginning of the fourth month the mouths of the depths of the abysses beneath were closed. And on the beginning of the seventh month**

all the mouths of the abysses of the earth were opened, and the waters began to descend into them. And on <u>the beginning of the tenth month</u> the tops of the mountains were seen and Noah was glad. And on this account he ordained them for himself as feast for a memorial forever, and thus they are they ordained. <u>And they placed them on the heavenly tables…thus it is engraven and ordained on the heavenly tables. And there is no neglecting this commandment for a single year or from year to year."</u> And command thou the children of Israel that they observe the years according to this reckoning- three hundred and sixty-four days, and (these) will constitute a complete year, and they will not disturb its time from its days and from its feast; for everything will fall out in them according to their testimony, and they will not leave out any day nor disturb any feasts. But if they do neglect and do not observe them according to His commandment, then they will disturb all their seasons, and the years will be dislodged from this (order), [and they will disturb the seasons and the years will be dislodged] and they will neglect their ordinances. And all the children of Israel will forget, and will not find the path of the years, and will forget the beginning of months, and seasons, and sabbaths, and they will go wrong as to all the order of the years. For I know and from henceforth shall I declare it unto thee, and it is not of my own devising; for the book (lieth) written before me, and on the heavenly tables the division of days is ordained, lest they forget the feasts of the covenant and walk according to the feasts of the Gentiles after their error and after their ignorance. <u>For there will be those who will assuredly make observations of the moon – now (it) disturbeth the seasons and cometh in from year to year ten days too soon. For this reason the years will come upon them when they will disturb (the order),</u> and make an abominable (day) the day of testimony, and an unclean day a feast day, and they will confound all the days, the holy with the unclean, and the unclean day with the holy; for they will go wrong as to the month and sabbaths and feasts and jubilees. For this reason I command and testify to thee that thou mayest testify to them; <u>for after thy death thy children will disturb (them), so that they will not make the year three hundred and sixty- four days only,</u> and for this reason they will go wrong as to the beginning of month and seasons and sabbaths and festivals, and they will eat all kinds of blood with all kinds of flesh."

Jubilees 4:16b- "…and he called his name Enoch. **And he was the first among men that are born on earth who learnt writing and knowledge and wisdom and who wrote down the signs of heaven according to the order of their months in a book, that men might know the seasons of the years according to thee order of their separate months.** And he was the first to write a testimony, and he testified to the sons of men among the generations of the earth, and recounted the weeks of the jubilees, and made known to them the days of the years, and set in order the months and recounted the Sabbaths of the years as we made (them) known to him. And what was and what will be he saw in a vision of his sleep, as it will happen to the children of men throughout their generations until the day of judgment; he saw and understood everything, and wrote his testimony, and placed the testimony on earth for all the children of men and for their generations…And he was moreover with the angels of YAH these six jubilees of years, **and they showed him everything which is on earth and in heavens, the rule of the sun, and he wrote down everything.**

Enoch 72:1 "The book of the courses of the luminaries of heaven, the relations of each, according to their name, origin, and months (dominion and seasons) which Uriel, the holy angel who was with me, who is their guide, showed me; and he showed me all their laws (regulations) exactly as they are, and how it is with each of the years of the world and to eternity, until the new creation is accomplished which endures until eternity."

Enoch 72:32 "On that day the night decreases and amounts to nine parts, and the day to nine parts, and the night is equal to the day and the year is exactly as it its days three hundred and sixty-four."

"On that day" – this day is known as the Spring Equinox

Enoch 74:12 "And the sun and the stars bring in all the years exactly, so that they do not advance or delay their position by a single day to eternity; but complete the years with perfect justice in 364 days."

Enoch 75:1-2 "And the leaders of the heads of the ten thousands, who are in charge of the whole creation and over all the stars, have also to do with the four days of the year which are not counted in the yearly calendar, being not separated from their office, according to the reckoning of the year, and these render service on the four days which are not counted in the reckoning of the year. And because of them men go wrong in them, for those luminaries truly render service to the stations of the world, one in the first door, one on the third door of heaven, one in the fourth door, and one in the sixth door, and the exactness of the year is accomplished through its separate three hundred and sixty-four stations."

Enoch 80:1 "And in those days the angel Uriel answered and said to me; 'Behold, I have shown you everything, Enoch, and I have revealed everything to you that you should see this sun and this moon, and the leaders of the stars of heaven and all those who turn them, their tasks and times and departures."

Enoch 81:1-2,5-6 "And he said to me: 'Enoch, look at these heavenly tablets and read what is written on them, and mark every individual fact.' And I looked at the heavenly tablets, and read everything which was written on it and understood everything, and read the book of all the deeds of mankind, and of all the children of flesh; that shall be on the earth to the end of generations…And the seven holy ones brought me and placed me on the earth before the door of my house, and said to me: 'Declare everything to your son Methuselah, and show to all your children that no flesh is righteous in the sight of the Lord, for He is their Creator. For one year we will leave you with your son, until you give your last commands, that you may teach your children and record it for them and testify to all your children; and in the second year they shall take you from their midst."

Enoch 82:1-7 "And now, my son Methuselah, all these things I am recounting to you and writing down for you! And I have revealed to you everything, and given you books concerning all these; so, my son Methuselah, preserve the books from your father's hand, and see that you deliver them to the generations of the world.

I have given wisdom to you and to your children, and those children to come, that they may give it to their children for generations. This wisdom namely that passes their understanding. And those who understand it shall not sleep, but shall listen that they may learn this wisdom, and it shall please those that eat thereof better than good food. Blessed are all the righteous, <u>blessed are all those who walk in the way of righteousness</u> and sin not as the sinners, <u>in the numbering of all their days in which the sun traverses heaven</u>, entering into and departing from the doors for <u>thirty days</u> with the heads of thousands of the order of the stars, <u>together with the four which are within the calendar which divide the four portions of the year,</u> which lead them and enter with them four days. Owing to them men shall be at fault and not count them in the whole number of days of the year. Men shall be at fault, and not recognize them accurately. For they belong to the calculations of the year and are truly recorded therein forever, one in the first door and one in the third, and one in the fourth and one in the sixth, <u>and the year is completed in three hundred and sixty-four days. And the account of it is accurate and the recorded counting thereof is exact; for the luminaries, and month and festivals, and years and days,</u> has Uriel shown and revealed to me, to whom the Lord of the whole creation of the world hath subjected the host of heaven."

Enoch 82:10 "Their four leaders who divide the four parts of the year enter first; and after them the <u>twelve leaders of the orders who divide the months;</u> and for three hundred and sixty days there are heads over thousands who divide the days, and for the four days in the calendar there are the leaders which divide the four parts of the year."

Enoch 82:14 "…In the beginning of the year Melkejal rises first and rules, who is named Tam'aini and sun, and all the days of his dominion while he bears rule are <u>ninety-one days.</u>"

Enoch 82:17 "The next leader after him is Hel'emmelek, whom one names the shining sun, and all the days of his light are <u>ninety-one days.</u>

Some teach that the four horses of Revelation rule the seasons and the constellations declare the month.

Enoch 74:12 "<u>And the sun and the stars bring in all the years exactly,</u> so that they do not advance or delay their position by a single day to eternity; but complete the years with perfect justice in 364 days."

The order is based on the meanings of the names of the sons of Yacov not their birthing order.

First Month – Naftali; constellation Aries Ruled by the White Horse; My Wrestling; Genesis 30:8 & 49:21

Second Month Yissichar; constellation Taurus Ruled by the White horse; Reward; Genesis 49:14,15

Third Month Shimeon; constellation Gemini Ruled by the White horse; Hear; Genesis 29:33 & 49:5-8

Fourth Month Yosef; constellation Cancer Ruled by the Red Horse; Added To; Genesis 30:24 & 49:22

Fifth Month Yahuda; constellation Leo Ruled by the Red Horse; Praise; Genesis 29:35 & 49:8

Sixth Month Asher; constellation Virgo Ruled by the Red Horse; Happy; Genesis 30:13 & 49:20

Seventh Month Levi; constellation Libra Ruled by the Black Horse; Attached; Genesis 49:5

Eighth Month -Dan; constellation Scorpio Ruled by the Black Horse; Judge; Genesis 30:6 & 49:17

Ninth Month - Gad; constellation Sagittarius Ruled by the Black Horse; Rider; Genesis 30:10 & 49:17

Tenth Month - BenYamin; constellation Capricorn; Pale Horse; Son of the Right Hand; Genesis 35:18 & 49:27

Eleventh Month - Reuben; constellation Aquarius Ruled by the Pale Horse; See A Son; Genesis 29:32 & 49:3

Twelfth Month - Zebulun; constellation Pisces Represented by the fish; Ruled by the Pale Horse; Exalted: Genesis 30:20; 49:13

I have noticed in my observation of the constellations each month that the 91 days between each season fluctuates although it works out in the end perfectly with 364 days. For example, on season can be 88 days and then next season can be 94 days, but the average remains 91. I have also noticed in my observation of time between Tekufa's (solstice's & equinoxes) that they are never more than a week off. The first day of the year is always the Wednesday during the Equinox, not after Spring Equinox week! I've seen some Zodiaks kept by Ancient Jews and they look like the sundials found in the Qumran caves for the calendar.

I'm not a fan of this section because I don't see how this information benefits us; however; science confirms that the constellations change every 30 days 12 times a year confirming 12 months of 30 days per year! Also these changes vary a little also, so you could have 27 days of one and 33 days of another but they all average out to 30 days of 12 months each. Basically science confirms what we have learned from the book of Enoch. Another point to understand is that the greater the distance away from the equator that the observer is will create a bigger fluctuation. So if you live on the equator you will not see the fluctuation, it will be more accurate so to speak- at least this is how I understand it to be in my one year of observation.

There are different lists attributing different months to the sons of Yacov- even though the names of the month vary, the fact remains that there are 12 months with 30 days each according to the 12 constellation of stars we can witness. I think the birthing order is the original order that they were in along with the zodiacal order of constellations which would be as follows: Rueben-Taurus, Simon-Gemini, Levi-Cancer, Judah-Leo, Zebulun-Virgo, Issachar-Libra, Dan-Scorpio, Gad-Sagittarius, Asher-Capricorn, Naphtali-Aquarius, Joseph-Pisces, Benjamin-Aries.

"A list the Creators Holidays"

Leviticus 23:1-4 / Jubilees 2:29 / Jubilees 50:6-13
1. **Sabbath/Shabbat** (Every Saturday which is the 7th day of the week) A commanded assembly day!

Numbers 28:1-15 / Genesis 8:13 / Exodus 12:4 & 13:4 / Jubilees 6:23-25 / Jubilees 7:2-3 / Jubilees 13:8

2. **Beginning of the First Month, Aviv, Head of Spring, Day of Remembrance**, Noah was told to build the ark and the earth dried up after the flood. The Spring Equinox is the Intercalary Day and is the 3rd day of the week, or on Tuesday, the last day of the year (364 days) and called the "Tekufa" in Hebrew. The Equinox is the Sign we are guard. Deuteronomy 16:1 "Guard the Sign of the month of the Aviv; and perform Passover, to YAHUAH your Elohim; Because in the month of the Aviv (season), YAHUAH your Elohim took you out of Egypt at night." RSTNE 7th Edition - The Sign being the Straight line at the Vernal Equinox! A commanded assembly day!

The First Day of every Torah month is a Commanded assembly. 2 Kings 4:23 "And he said why will you go to him today? It is neither a new month nor a Sabbath. And she said it will be well". The Kings of Israel would always meet the prophets at a Gilgal on the Feast Days and on the heads of the months. They gathered to hear the prophets on the beginning of the new month and every Sabbath.

Leviticus 23:5
3. **YAH's Passover/Pesach** (Aviv 14th Exodus 13:4 (Nisan - pagan name) usually between March and April). I think this is more of a family gathering rather than a congregational assembly.

Leviticus 23:6-8
4. **Feast of Unleavened Bread** (Aviv 15th for **7 days**). The first and last day of Unleavened Bread is a commanded assembly day!

Leviticus 23:9-14

5. First Fruits (Aviv 26th this is the day after the weekly Sabbath, the week after Unleavened Bread. **This is the Barley Harvest.** Begin counting this day to the next First Fruits Harvest – 50 days!) All first fruits harvest land on the first day of the week! It's called the counting of the Omer. I think assembly is implied.

Leviticus 23:15-22

6. Pentecost/Feast of Weeks/Shavuot (3rd Month 15th Day, 50 days after First Fruits.) **This is the first fruits of the Wheat Harvest.** Begin counting this day to the next First Fruits Harvest. The book of Jasher 82:6 has the ten commandments being given on the sixth day of the 3rd month and it is said that the 10 commandments were given on Shavuot. However, the Enoch calendar has Shavuot on the 15th of the third month. All first fruits harvest land on the first day of the week! I think assembly is implied.

Genesis 8:2 / Jubilees 6:26

7. Beginning of the Fourth Month (Head of Summer), **Day of Remembrance;** the mouth of the waters of the depth were closed after the flood. The Summer Solstice is the Intercalary Day the day before the beginning of the fourth month. In Hebrew it's called the Tekufa. A commanded assembly day!

Exodus 34:22 / Deuteronomy 18:4 / Jubilees 7:36 / Found on the Calendar at Qumran Caves

8. Pentecost/Feast of Weeks/Shavuot (5th Month 3rd Day) **This is the first fruits of New Wine.** Begin counting this day to the next First Fruits Harvest. All first fruits harvests land on the first day of the week. I think assembly is implied.

Jubilees 7:36 / Exodus 34:22/ Deuteronomy 18:4 / Found on the Calendar at Qumran Caves

9. Pentecost/Feast of Weeks/Shavuot (6th Month 22nd Day) **This is the First Fruits of New Oil.** This is the last of the First Fruits Harvests for the year. All first fruits harvests land on the first day of the week. I think assembly is implied.

Leviticus 23:23-25 / Jubilees 6:26

10. **Feast of Trumpets/Blowing of Trumpets/Yom Teruah** (Ethanim 1st I Kings 8:2 (Tishri-pagan name)) **Beginning of the 7th month, Head of Fall, Day of Remembrance,** all the mouths of the abysses of the earth were opened, and the waters began to descend into them. The Fall Equinox is the Intercalary Day, the day before the Beginning of the seventh month. In Hebrew they call it the Tekufa. A commanded assembly day.

Leviticus 23:26-32 / Jubilees 5:18 / Jubilees 34 / Jubilees 34:18-19

11. **Day of Atonement/ Yom Kippur** (Ethanim 10th) Considered by many to be the most consecrated set apart day; I have seen in scripture that the word for the weekly Sabbath and the word for this Annual Sabbath are the same. The word for all the other Sabbaths is different. So Scripture makes a distinction, but I'm not for sure what the difference is. Sabbath and Yom Kippur are days of no work at all; and the other feast days Sabbathowns are more lenient with the work you do, but still no occupational work. A commanded assembly day.

Leviticus 23:33-44 / Jubilees 16 & 32

12. **Feast of Tabernacles/Feast of Booths/Sukkot** (Ethanim 15th for **8 days**). This is actually for 7 days and then there is the 8th day which seems to be distinct and separate in itself. A commanded assembly required on the 15th and 22nd day of the month.

Genesis 8:5 / Jubilees 6:27

13. **Beginning of the Tenth Month (Head of Winter), Day of Remembrance,** mountain tops were seen after the flood as Noah rejoiced. The Intercalary Day is the winter solstice, which should occur the day before the Beginning of the Tenth Month. In Hebrew they have one word for the equinoxes and solstices, it is Tekufa. A commanded assembly day.

I will add Purim and Hanukkah to the calendar as well since they are clearly part of the history of Israel and Purim is in the book of Esther and Hannukah is in the book of Maccabees.

Maccabbees 4:54,56,59 "Then all the people fell upon their faces, worshipping and praising the Alahim of heaven, who had given them good success. And so they kept the dedication of the altar eight days, and offered burnt offerings with gladness, and sacrificed the sacrifice of deliverance and praise…Moreover Judas and his brethren with the whole congregation of Israel ordained, that the days of the dedication of the altar should be kept in their season from year to year by the space of eight days, from the five and twentieth day of the month Casleu, with mirth and gladness."

Hanukkah is **celebrated for eight days and it begins on** the 25th of Kislev or **the 9th scriptural month** and it ends on the Beginning of the 10th month.

Esther 9:17, 18, 21 – In the month of Adar on the 14th day and the 15th day they rested and made it a day of feasting and rejoicing. **Esther 9:26-32**

Purim is celebrated on the 14th and 15th day of the 12th month.

Names of the Months found in Scripture

First Month- Aviv, Abib, the green leaf, green ripe ears. Exodus 12:2 and 13:4- It's also called Nisan in Esther 3:7. So to me it looks like in Persian captivity Israel changed the name to Nisan adopting a pagan name. This green leaf is referring to spring and it would be the barley harvest in Israel.

Second Month- Ziv, Zif, blossom, month of flowers. I Kings 6:1,37

Third Month- Sivan, Esther 8:9 - this word is probably of Persian origin.

Fourth Month- Tammuz, Ezekiel 8:14 - well you can't get any more pagan than this.

Fifth Month- Av, Ab, this name isn't even found in scripture to my knowledge.

Sixth Month- Elul, Nehemiah (Nekem Yah) 6:15 - Since Strongs concordance gives no definition for this word and it's after Babylonian captivity, it's probably an improper name for the month.

Seventh Moth- Ethanim, I Kings 8:2- A constancy of Streams or the permanent brooks. Tishri is probably a pagan name and not found in Scripture either as far as I know.

Eighth Month- Bul, I Kings 6:38 - as in the sense of Rain.

Ninth Month- Chislev, Kislev, Nehemiah 1:1; Zechariah 7:1- BDB pg 493 B says Kisleu is a loan word from Babylon.

Tenth Month- Tebeth, Esther 2:16- Not of Hebrew origin.

Eleventh Month- Shebat, Zechariah (Zakar Yahu) 1:7- Babylonian word.

Twelfth Month- Adar, Esther 3:7- Another loan word from Babylon.

First Month – 5947 A.M.

March/April 2022 A.D.

DiscipleMakingPastor.org/Enochian/Dead Sea Scroll Essene/Zadokite/Torah/Solar/364 Day Year/Creators Calendar

Day 1	Day 2	Day 3	Day 4	Day 5	Day 6	SHABBAT
Spring Equinox	Rueben Pisces		**1st Month Day 1 Head of Spring, Day of Remembrance** March 23	1st Month Day 2 March 24	1st Month Day 3 March 25	1st Month Day 4 March 26
1st Month Day 5 March 27	1st Month Day 6 March 28	1st Month Day 7 March 29	1st Month Day 8 March 30	1st Month Day 9 March 31	1st Month Day 10 April 1	1st Month Day 11 April 2
1st Month Day 12 April 3	1st Month Day 13 April 4	**1st Month Day 14 Passover Pesach April 5**	**1st Month Day 15 Unleavened Bread Day 1 Assembly April 6**	**1st Month Day 16 Unleavened Bread Day 2 April 7**	**1st Month Day 17 Unleavened Bread Day 3 April 8**	**1st Month Day 18 Unleavened Bread Day 4 Resurrection Morning!!! April 9**
1st Month Day 19 Unleavened Bread Day 5 April 10	**1st Month Day 20 Unleavened Bread Day 6 April 11**	**1st Month Day 21 Unleavened Bread Day 7 Assembly April 12**	1st Month Day 22 April 13	1st Month Day 23 April 14	1st Month Day 24 April 15	1st Month Day 25 April 16
1st Month Day 26 First Fruits of Barley Omer Count Begins April 17	1st Month Day 27 April 18	1st Month Day 28 April 19	1st Month Day 29 April 20	1st Month Day 30 April 21		

Second Month – 5947 A.M.

April / May 2022 A.D.

DiscipleMakingPastor.org/Enochian/Dead Sea Scroll
Essene/Zadokite/Torah/Solar/364 Day Year/Creators Calendar

Day 1	Day 2	Day 3	Day 4	Day 5	Day 6	SHABBAT
				Simeon Aries	**2nd Month Day 1 Beginning of Second Month** **April 22**	2nd Month Day 2 Omer – 7 April 23
2nd Month Day 3 April 24	2nd Month Day 4 April 25	2nd Month Day 5 April 26	2nd Month Day 6 April 27	2nd Month Day 7 April 28	2nd Month Day 8 April 29	2nd Month Day 9 Omer – 14 April 30
2nd Month Day 10 May 1	2nd Month Day 11 May 2	2nd Month Day 12 May 3	2nd Month Day 13 May 4	**2nd Month Day 14 2nd Passover/ Pesach** **May 5**	2nd Month Day 15 May 6	2nd Month Day 16 Omer – 21 May 7
2nd Month Day 17 Gen.7:11 Flood Begins! May 8	2nd Month Day 18 May 9	2nd Month Day 19 May 10	2nd Month Day 20 May 11	2nd Month Day 21 May 12	2nd Month Day 22 May 13	2nd Month Day 23 Omer – 28 May 14
2nd Month Day 24 May 15	2nd Month Day 25 May 16	2nd Month Day 26 May 17	2nd Month Day 27 May 18	2nd Month Day 28 May 19	2nd Month Day 29 May 20	2nd Month Day 30 Omer – 35 May 21

Third Month – 5947 A.M.

May / June 2022 A.D.

DiscipleMakingPastor.org/Enochian/Dead Sea Scroll
Essene/Zadokite/Torah/Solar/364 Day Year/Creators Calendar

Day 1	Day 2	Day 3	Day 4	Day 5	Day 6	SHABBAT
3rd Month Day 1 **Head of the Month** **May 22**	3rd Month Day 2 Levi Aries May 23	3rd Month Day 3 May 24	3rd Month Day 4 May 25	3rd Month Day 5 May 26	3rd Month Day 6 May 27	3rd Month Day 7 Omer – 42 May 28
3rd Month Day 8 May 29	3rd Month Day 9 May 30	3rd Month Day 10 May 31	3rd Month Day 11 June 1	3rd Month Day 12 June 2	3rd Month Day 13 June 3	3rd Month Day 14 Omer – 49 June 4
3rd Month Day 15 Shavuot, First Fruits of Wheat, Pentecost June 5	3rd Month Day 16 June 6	3rd Month Day 17 June 7	3rd Month Day 18 June 8	3rd Month Day 19 June 9	3rd Month Day 20 June 10	3rd Month Day 21 New Wine – 7 June 11
3rd Month Day 22 June 12	3rd Month Day 23 June 13	3rd Month Day 24 June 14	3rd Month Day 25 June 15	3rd Month Day 26 June 16	3rd Month Day 27 June 17	3rd Month Day 28 New Wine - 14 June 18
3rd Month Day 29 June 19	3rd Month Day 30 June 20	Intercalary Day 31 Summer Solstice Tekufa June 21	**4th Month Day 1 Head of Summer, Day of Remembrance** **June 22**			

Fourth Month – 5947 A.M.

June/July 2022 A.D.

DiscipleMakingPastor.org/Enochian/Dead Sea Scroll
Essene/Zadokite/Torah/Solar/364 Day Year/Creators Calendar

Day 1	Day 2	Day 3	Day 4	Day 5	Day 6	SHABBAT
	Gemini Judah	Intercalary Day 31 Summer Solstice Tekufa	**4th Month Day 1 Head of Summer/ Day of Remembrance June 22**	4th Month Day 2 June 23	4th Month Day 3 June 24	4th Month Day 4 New Wine - 21 June 25
4th Month Day 5 June 26	4th Month Day 6 June 27	4th Month Day 7 Summer Solstice June 28	4th Month Day 8 June 29	4th Month Day 9 June 30	4th Month Day 10 July 1	4th Month Day 11 New Wine - 28 July 2
4th Month Day 12 July 3	4th Month Day 13 July 4	4th Month Day 14 July 5	4th Month Day 15 July 6	4th Month Day 16 July 7	4th Month Day 17 July 8	4th Month Day 18 New Wine – 35 July 9
4th Month Day 19 July 10	4th Month Day 20 July 11	4th Month Day 21 July 12	4th Month Day 22 July 13	4th Month Day 23 July 14	4th Month Day 24 July 15	4th Month Day 25 New Wine – 42 July 16
4th Month Day 26 July 17	4th Month Day 27 July 18	4th Month Day 28 July 19	4th Month Day 29 July 20	4th Month Day 30 July 21		

Fifth Month – 5947 A.M.

July / August 2022 A.D.

DiscipleMakingPastor.org/Enochian/Dead Sea Scroll
Essene/Zadokite/Torah/Solar/364 Day Year/Creators Calendar

Day 1	Day 2	Day 3	Day 4	Day 5	Day 6	SHABBAT
				Cancer Zebulun	**5th Month** **Day 1** **Head of the Month** **July 22**	5th Month Day 2 New Wine - 49 July 23
5th Month **Day 3** **First Fruits of New Wine** **Day 50** **July 24**	5th Month Day 4 July 25	5th Month Day 5 July 26	5th Month Day 6 July 27	5th Month Day 7 July 28	5th Month Day 8 July 29	5th Month Day 9 New Oil - 7 July 30
5th Month Day 10 July 31	5th Month Day 11 August 1	5th Month Day 12 August 2	5th Month Day 13 August 3	5th Month Day 14 August 4	5th Month Day 15 August 5	5th Month Day 16 New Oil - 14 August 6
5th Month Day 17 August 7	5th Month Day 18 August 8	5th Month Day 19 August 9	5th Month Day 20 August 10	5th Month Day 21 August 11	5th Month Day 22 August 12	5th Month Day 23 New Oil - 21 August 13
5th Month Day 24 August 14	5th Month Day 25 August 15	5th Month Day 26 August 16	5th Month Day 27 August 17	5th Month Day 28 August 18	5th Month Day 29 August 19	5th Month Day 30 New Oil - 28 August 20

Sixth Month – 5947 A.M.
August / September 2022 A.D.

DiscipleMakingPastor.org/Enochian/Dead Sea Scroll
Essene/Zadokite/Torah/Solar/364 Day Year/Creators Calendar

Day 1	Day 2	Day 3	Day 4	Day 5	Day 6	SHABBAT
6th Month Day 1 Head of the Month August 21	6th Month Day 2 Issachar Leo August 22	6th Month Day 3 August 23	6th Month Day 4 August 24	6th Month Day 5 August 25	6th Month Day 6 August 26	6th Month Day 7 New Oil - 35 August 27
6th Month Day 8 August 28	6th Month Day 9 August 29	6th Month Day 10 August 30	6th Month Day 11 August 31	6th Month Day 12 September 1	6th Month Day 13 September 2	6th Month Day 14 New Oil - 42 September 3
6th Month Day 15 September 4	6th Month Day 16 September 5	6th Month Day 17 September 6	6th Month Day 18 September 7	6th Month Day 19 September 8	6th Month Day 20 September 9	6th Month Day 21 New Oil - 49 September 10
6th Month Day 22 First Fruits of New Oil Day 50 September 11	6th Month Day 23 Wood Offering September 12	6th Month Wood Offering September 13	6th Month Day 25 Wood Offering September 14	6th Month Day 26 Wood Offering September 15	6th Month Wood Offering September 16	6th Month Day 28 September 17
6th Month Day 29 The Wood Offering Closing Assembly September 18	6th Month Day 30 September 19	Intercalary Day 31 Fall Equinox Tekufa September 20	**7th Month Day 1 Head of Fall/ A Day of Remembrance Trumpets/ Assembly** September 21			

Seventh Month – 5947 A.M.

September / October 2022 A.D.

DiscipleMakingPastor.org/Enochian/Dead Sea Scroll
Essene/Zadokite/Torah/Solar/364 Day Year/Creators Calendar

Day 1	Day 2	Day 3	Day 4	Day 5	Day 6	SHABBAT
	Virgo Dan	Intercalary Day 31 Fall Equinox Tekufa September 20	7th Month Day 1 Head of Fall/ A Day of Remembrance Trumpets/ Assembly September 21	7th Month Day 2 September 22	7th Month Day 3 September 23	7th Month Day 4 September 24
7th Month Day 5 September 25	7th Month Day 6 September 26	7th Month Day 7 September 27	7th Month Day 8 September 28	7th Month Day 9 Fall Equinox September 29	7th Month Day 10 Yom Kippur Day of Atonement Assembly September 30	7th Month Day 11 October 1
7th Month Day 12 October 2	7th Month Day 13 October 3	7th Month Day 14 October 4	7th Month Day 15 Sukkot Feast of Tabernacles Assembly October 5	7th Month Day 16 Sukkot Feast of Tabernacles October 6	7th Month Day 17 Sukkot Feast of Tabernacles October 7	7th Month Day 18 Sukkot Feast of Tabernacles October 8
7th Month Day 19 Sukkot Feast of Tabernacles October 9	7th Month Day 20 Sukkot Feast of Tabernacles October 10	7th Month Day 21 Last Great Day of Tabernacles October 11	7th Month Day 22 Eight Day Assembly October 12	7th Month Day 23 October 13	7th Month Day 24 October 14	7th Month Day 25 October 15
7th Month Day 26 October 16	7th Month Day 27 October 17	7th Month Day 28 October 1	7th Month Day 29 October 19	7th Month Day 30 October 20		

Eighth Month – 5947 A.M.

October / November 2022 A.D.

DiscipleMakingPastor.org/Enochian/Dead Sea Scroll
Essene/Zadokite/Torah/Solar/364 Day Year/Creators Calendar

Day 1	Day 2	Day 3	Day 4	Day 5	Day 6	SHABBAT
				Libra Gad	8th Month Day 1 October 21	8th Month Day 2 October 22
8th Month Day 3 October 23	8th Month Day 4 October 24	8th Month Day 5 October 25	8th Month Day 6 October 26	8th Month Day 7 October 27	8th Month Day 8 October 28	8th Month Day 9 October 29
8th Month Day 10 October 30	8th Month Day 11 October 31	8th Month Day 12 November 1	8th Month Day 13 November 2	8th Month Day 14 November 3	8th Month Day 15 November 4	8th Month Day 16 November 5
8th Month Day 17 November 6	8th Month Day 18 November 7	8th Month Day 19 November 8	8th Month Day 20 November 9	8th Month Day 21 November 10	8th Month Day 22 November 11	8th Month Day 23 November 12
8th Month Day 24 November 13	8th Month Day 25 November 14	8th Month Day 26 November 15	8th Month Day 27 November 16	8th Month Day 28 November 17	8th Month Day 29 November 18	8th Month Day 30 November 19

Ninth Month – 5947 A.M.

November / December 2022 A.D.

DiscipleMakingPastor.org/Enochian/Dead Sea Scroll Essene/Zadokite/Torah/Solar/364 Day Year/Creators Calendar

Day 1	Day 2	Day 3	Day 4	Day 5	Day 6	SHABBAT
9th Month Day 1 Asher Scorpio November 20	9th Month Day 2 November 21	9th Month Day 3 November 22	9th Month Day 4 November 23	9th Month Day 5 November 24	9th Month Day 6 November 25	9th Month Day 7 November 26
9th Month Day 8 November 27	9th Month Day 9 November 28	9th Month Day 10 November 29	9th Month Day 11 November 30	9th Month Day 12 December 1	9th Month Day 13 December 2	9th Month Day 14 December 3
9th Month Day 15 December 4	9th Month Day 16 December 5	9th Month Day 17 December 6	9th Month Day 18 December 7	9th Month Day 19 December 8	9th Month Day 20 December 9	9th Month Day 21 December 10
9th Month Day 22 December 11	9th Month Day 23 December 12	9th Month Day 24 December 13	9th Month Day 25 **1st day of Chanukkah** December 14	9th Month Day 26 **2nd day of Chanukkah** December 15	9th Month Day 27 **3rd day of Chanukkah** December 16	9th Month Day 28 **4th day of Chanukkah** December 17
9th Month Day 29 **5th day of Chanukah** December 18	9th Month Day 30 **6th day of Chanukkah** December 19	Intercalary Day 31, Winter Solstice, Tekufa **7th day of Chanukkah** December 20	**10th Month Day 1, Head of Winter, Day of Remembrance 8th day of Chanukkah** **December 21**			

24

Tenth Month – 5947 A.M.

December 2022 A.D. / January 2023 A.D.

DiscipleMakingPastor.org/Enochian/Dead Sea Scroll
Essene/Zadokite/Torah/Solar/364 Day Year/Creators Calendar

Day 1	Day 2	Day 3	Day 4	Day 5	Day 6	SHABBAT
	Sagittarius Naphtali	Intercalary Day 31, Winter Solstice, Tekufa December 20	**10th Month Day 1, Head of Winter, Day of Remembrance 8th day Chanukkah December 21**	10th Month Day 2 December 22	10th Month Day 3 December 23	10th Month Day 4 December 24
10th Month Day 5 December 25	10th Month Day 6 December 26	10th Month Day 7 December 27	10th Month Day 8 Winter Solstice December 28	10th Month Day 9 December 29	10th Month Day 10 December 30	10th Month Day 11 December 31
10th Month Day 12 January 1	10th Month Day 13 January 2	10th Month Day 14 January 3	10th Month Day 15 January 4	10th Month Day 16 January 5	10th Month Day 17 January 6	10th Month Day 18 January 7
10th Month Day 19 January 8	10th Month Day 20 January 9	10th Month Day 21 January 10	10th Month Day 22 January 11	10th Month Day 23 January 12	10th Month Day 24 January 13	10th Month Day 25 January 14
10th Month Day 26 January 15	10th Month Day 27 January 16	10th Month Day 28 January 17	10th Month Day 29 January 18	10th Month Day 30 January 19		

Eleventh Month – 5947 A.M.

January / February 2023 A.D.

DiscipleMakingPastor.org/Enochian/Dead Sea Scroll
Essene/Zadokite/Torah/Solar/364 Day Year/Creators Calendar

Day 1	Day 2	Day 3	Day 4	Day 5	Day 6	SHABBAT
				Capicorn Yoseph	11th Month Day 1 January 20	11th Month Day 2 January 21
11th Month Day 3 January 22	11th Month Day 4 January 23	11th Month Day 5 January 24	11th Month Day 6 January 25	11th Month Day 7 January 26	11th Month Day 8 January 27	11th Month Day 9 January 28
11th Month Day 10 January 29	11th Month Day 11 January 30	11th Month Day 12 January 31	11th Month Day 13 February 1	11th Month Day 14 February 2	11th Month Day 15 February 3	11th Month Day 16 February 4
11th Month Day 17 February 5	11th Month Day 18 February 6	11th Month Day 19 February 7	11th Month Day 20 February 8	11th Month Day 21 February 9	11th Month Day 22 February 10	11th Month Day 23 February 11
11th Month Day 24 February 12	11th Month Day 25 February 13	11th Month Day 26 February 14	11th Month Day 27 February 15	11th Month Day 28 February 16	11th Month Day 29 February 17	11th Month Day 30 February 18

Twelfth Month – 5947 A.M.

February / March 2023 A.D.

DiscipleMakingPastor.org/Enochian/Dead Sea Scroll
Essene/Zadokite/Torah/Solar/364 Day Year/Creators Calendar

Day 1	Day 2	Day 3	Day 4	Day 5	Day 6	SHABBAT
12th Month Day 1 Benjamin Aquarius February 19	12th Month Day 2 February 20	12th Month Day 3 February 21	12th Month Day 4 February 22	12th Month Day 5 February 23	12th Month Day 6 February 24	12th Month Day 7 February 25
12th Month Day 8 February 26	12th Month Day 9 February 27	12th Month Day 10 February 28	12th Month Day 11 March 1	12th Month Day 12 March 2	12th Month Day 13 March 3	12th Month Day 14 March 4
12th Month Day 15 March 5	12th Month Day 16 March 6	12th Month Day 17 March 7	12th Month Day 18 March 8	12th Month Day 19 March 9	12th Month Day 20 March 10	12th Month Day 21 March 11
12th Month Day 22 March 12	12th Month Day 23 March 13	12th Month Day 24 March 14	12th Month Day 25 March 15	12th Month Day 26 March 16	12th Month Day 27 March 17	12th Month Day 28 March 18
12th Month Day 29 March 19	12th Month Day 30 Spring Equinox March 20	Intercalary Day 31 Tekufa, Spring Equinox, Day 364 Count Stops March 21	**1st Month Day 1 Head of Spring NewYear5948 Day of Remembrance March 22**	March 23	March 24	March 25

Ingram Content Group UK Ltd.
Milton Keynes UK
UKHW030633130723
425071UK00012B/358